THE BEGINNER'S BIBLE

My
Promise
Bible

™

The Beginners Bible—My Promise Bible
ISBN 1-56292-933-X

Published by Honor Books
P. O. Box 55388
Tulsa, Oklahoma 74155

Introduction

The Bible is a book full of wonderful stories and promises. God promises to love you and be with you no matter what. He promises to help you and lead you. He promises to watch over you and care for you. He promises to be your best friend. God says you are never alone.

My Promise Bible begins with the story of how people were created in the Garden of Eden. Then you will read about Noah and Abraham and Moses, all ordinary people who listened to and obeyed an extraordinary God. One of the best stories of all is about God's son, Jesus Christ!

There's no better time to read about God's promises than at bedtime. Just knowing that he loves you and watches over you will help you sleep peacefully. And during the day, you can read and remember how God has promised to always take care of you.

God loves you very much. And you will learn to love him more and more each day as you read *My Promise Bible*.

Table of Contents

Caring for
the Garden

● ●

God made the earth and the sky. He made the moon and all the stars that shine at night. God made the rivers and the oceans. He made mountains and valleys. He made clouds and trees. Then God made all the animals. He made tiny ants and big elephants. He made eagles that fly and whales that swim.

After God made all these things, God made a man.

Today's Promise

God gave Adam and Eve everything they needed in the garden. He took good care of them. God promises to take care of me, too.

9

His name was Adam. God made a home for Adam in a beautiful garden. The garden was filled with every kind of plant and tree. There were tall trees and short trees. There were green plants and colorful flowers. God made fruit trees so Adam would have plenty of food to eat.

Then God gave Adam a very important job. Adam cared for the garden and everything in it. Finally, God made a woman to be Adam's partner in the garden. Her name was Eve. She helped Adam care for the garden that God had made.

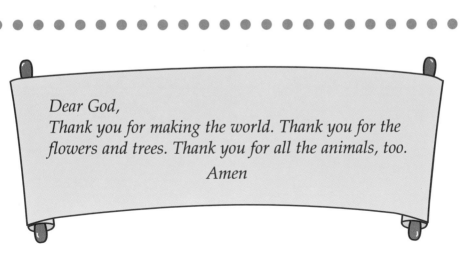

Dear God,
Thank you for making the world. Thank you for the flowers and trees. Thank you for all the animals, too.
Amen

The Great Flood

Genesis 6:9

● ●

L ong ago, most of the people in the world did not love God. They were not kind to each other. God searched the world to find one good person. He found a man named Noah who worshiped him. God told Noah that he was going to flood the earth, but Noah and his family would be safe. God gave Noah instructions for building a big boat called an ark.

Today's Promise

Noah and his family loved God very much. God saved them from the flood. God promises to watch over me, too.

Noah and his family began building the ark right away. They worked until the ark was finished.

God sent two of every animal to Noah. Noah and his family loaded the animals onto the ark.

Then God sent rain. The rain fell for many days. Finally, the rain stopped. The flood covered everything. But Noah, his family, and the animals were safe.

One day, Noah sent a raven to fly around and look for dry land. But the raven could not find land. Then

Noah sent out a dove. The dove brought back a leaf from an olive tree. This meant that the water was going down. Later, Noah sent out another dove. This time, the dove did not return. It had found a dry place to stay.

The ark stopped on top of a mountain. Everyone left the ark. Noah and his family thanked God for saving them.

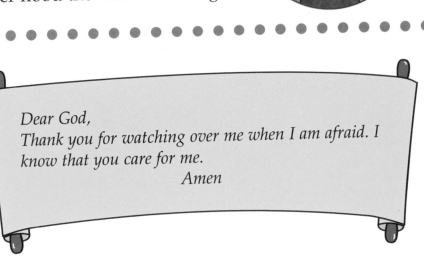

Then God placed a big rainbow in the sky. This was a sign from God that he would never flood the whole earth again.

Dear God,
Thank you for watching over me when I am afraid. I know that you care for me.
Amen

Abraham's New Home

Genesis 12:1

• •

Abraham and his family lived in a place called Haran. They had lived there for many years. But God had special plans for Abraham. One day, God told Abraham to move his family to a land called Canaan. Abraham loved God and trusted him. So Abraham, his wife, Sarah, and his nephew, Lot, packed up all of their belongings. Then they made the long

Today's Promise

Abraham trusted God to do what was best for him. God promises to lead and guide my family and me, too.

journey to their new home.

After they reached Canaan, Abraham divided the land with Lot. He allowed Lot to choose the part of Canaan he wanted for his home. Lot chose the best land and moved away from Abraham.

God made Abraham a promise. His family would grow to be a special group of people someday. And he would lead them to become a great nation.

But Abraham and his wife had no children. And they believed that they were too old to have children. But God kept his promise. Later, Abraham and Sarah had a son. They named him Isaac.

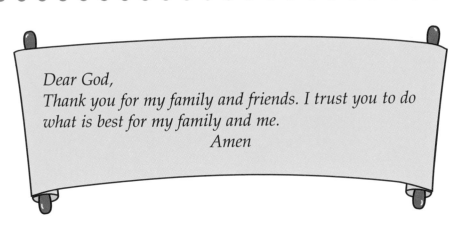

Dear God,
Thank you for my family and friends. I trust you to do
what is best for my family and me.
Amen

Isaac Gets Married

Genesis 24:10

Isaac was very sad. His mother had just died. His father, Abraham, decided that he should get married. Abraham told his servant to take a journey and search for a woman to be Isaac's wife.

One day, the servant found a well where he could get water for his camels. Then he prayed to God for help. If a woman offered to get water for his camels, he

Today's Promise

Abraham's servant had faith in God. And God helped him find a wife for Isaac. God promises to hear my prayers, too.

would know that she was God's choice.

A beautiful young woman named Rebekah came to the well. She was very kind to the servant. She offered to give water to his camels. God had answered his prayer. The servant explained to her why he had come.

Rebekah told her father what had happened. Her father knew Abraham. He happily allowed her to go with the servant to meet Isaac. So she returned with Abraham's servant. When Isaac met Rebekah, he instantly fell in love with her. With God's help, Isaac married Rebekah.

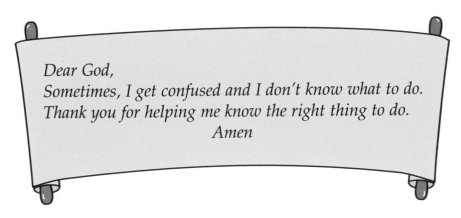

Dear God,
Sometimes, I get confused and I don't know what to do.
Thank you for helping me know the right thing to do.
Amen

Joseph's New Coat

Genesis 37:3

● ●

Jacob had twelve sons. Joseph was his favorite. One day, Jacob gave Joseph a special gift. It was a beautiful coat that Jacob had made.

Joseph loved his new coat. He showed it to his brothers. This made them very angry because they did not get new coats.

One night, Joseph had a strange dream. Joseph told

Today's Promise

God had a special plan for Joseph's life. God says he has a special plan for my life, too. He promises to help me follow his plan.

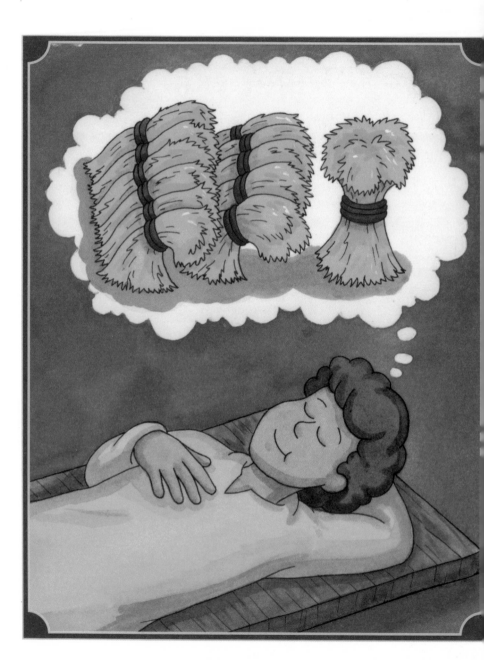

his brothers about his dream. They knew what the dream meant. According to the dream, they would bow down to Joseph someday. This made Joseph's brothers so angry that they decided to get rid of him.

Later, Joseph's brothers were working in the field. Joseph came to see them. They grabbed Joseph and sold him to some traders who were going to Egypt. Then the brothers tricked Jacob. They made him believe that Joseph had been killed by a wild animal. But God was watching over Joseph. God had special plans for him.

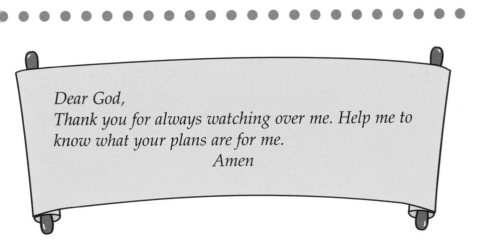

Dear God,
Thank you for always watching over me. Help me to know what your plans are for me.
Amen

Pharaoh's Dream

Genesis 41:14

● ●

Joseph's brothers did not like him. They sold him to a group of traders. Then the traders took Joseph to Egypt. They sold him to Pharaoh's captain of the guards. The captain placed Joseph in Pharaoh's prison. Joseph was locked up in prison for a long time. But Joseph always trusted God to take care of him.

With God's help, Joseph could tell other people what

Today's Promise

Joseph knew God would watch over him, even when he had lots of troubles in his life. And God promises to take care of me when I have bad days.

their dreams meant. One day, Pharaoh had a strange dream. He had heard about Joseph's special talent. He called for Joseph and told him about the dream. In his dream, seven skinny cows swallowed seven fat cows.

Joseph explained the dream to him. Egypt would have seven years with good weather and plenty of crops to feed everyone. But then there would be seven years of bad weather when nothing would grow. Pharaoh believed Joseph and released him from prison. Then he gave Joseph an important job in his palace.

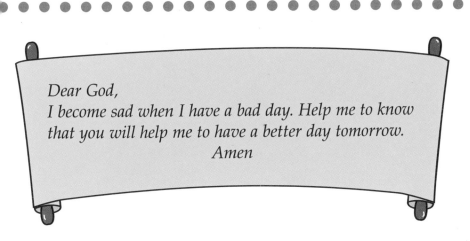

Dear God,
I become sad when I have a bad day. Help me to know that you will help me to have a better day tomorrow.
Amen

Joseph's Brothers

Genesis 42:1-2

• •

Joseph had become an important person in Pharaoh's palace. He had warned Pharaoh that there was going to be a seven year drought. So Pharaoh gave Joseph a big job. Joseph was in charge of collecting and storing grain for food. Then, during the dry spell, there would be enough food to feed everyone.

The drought came just as Joseph had said. People

Today's Promise

Joseph did not hate his brothers for selling him to traders. He forgave them. God promises to forgive me, too.

came to Egypt to buy grain because they could not grow their own food.

Joseph's father, Jacob, sent his sons to Egypt to buy grain. They met Joseph and bowed down to him. They did not know that he was their brother whom they had sold many years before.

Joseph told them that he was their brother, Joseph. They were afraid that he would punish them for what they had done. But Joseph forgave them. Then he invited his brothers to return with Jacob to live in Egypt with him.

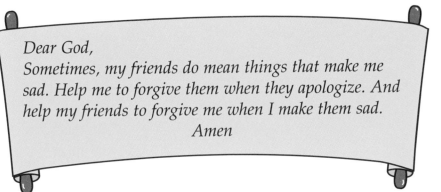

Dear God,
Sometimes, my friends do mean things that make me sad. Help me to forgive them when they apologize. And help my friends to forgive me when I make them sad.
Amen

Baby Moses Is Saved

Exodus 2:1-2

Egypt's new ruler did not like the Israelites who lived in Egypt. He was cruel to them. He made them work very hard for him every day. One day, Pharaoh decided to get rid of any Israelite baby boys born in Egypt.

One woman had a plan to save her baby boy. She found a basket and covered it with tar so that it would

Today's Promise

Moses' mother saved him because she loved him very much. God promises to love my family and take care of us, too.

float. She placed her baby in the basket and put the basket in the river. Her daughter followed the basket as it floated away.

Pharaoh's daughter walked down to the river and found the baby. She named him Moses and planned to keep him. Moses' sister told her she knew a woman who would care for the baby until he was older. The woman was Moses' own mother!

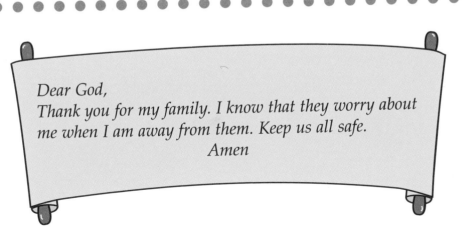

Pharaoh's daughter agreed. Moses' mother cared for him for many years. Then she returned him to the palace to live with Pharaoh's daughter.

Dear God,
Thank you for my family. I know that they worry about me when I am away from them. Keep us all safe.
Amen

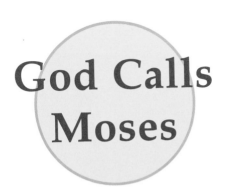

God Calls Moses

Exodus 3:1

• •

Moses spent part of his childhood at Pharaoh's palace in Egypt. But when he grew up, Moses left Egypt and settled in Midian. He became a shepherd and married a woman who lived there.

One day, Moses was watching his family's flock of sheep. Suddenly, he saw a bush that was on fire. But the fire did not burn the bush. God called to Moses

Today's Promise

Moses obeyed God. He left his home and returned to Egypt to help his people. I want to obey God, too. God promises to help me know what to do.

43

from the bush. God told him that his people were still slaves in Egypt. Pharaoh was treating them very badly.

God told Moses to go to Egypt and help his people gain their freedom. After they were free, God would lead them to a new land where they would make their new home.

But Moses did not believe that he would be a good leader. God promised to help him. God chose Moses' brother, Aaron, to go with him to see Pharaoh in Egypt. Moses obeyed God. He and his family left their home and traveled to Egypt.

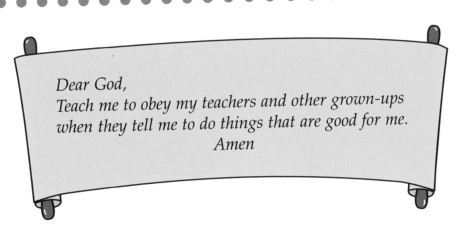

Dear God,
Teach me to obey my teachers and other grown-ups when they tell me to do things that are good for me.
                                        Amen

Moses Returns to Egypt

Exodus 5:1

Moses and his brother, Aaron, went to see Pharaoh at his palace. They told Pharaoh that God had brought them to Egypt to lead the Israelite slaves to freedom.

But Pharaoh did not worship God. He refused to let the slaves go free. Instead, Pharaoh made the slaves work even harder than before.

Today's Promise

Moses trusted God to help him free his people from slavery. God wants me to trust him, too. He promises to help my friends and me when we have problems.

God told Moses what to do. Moses and Aaron went to see Pharaoh again. Aaron threw his walking stick down on the ground. Suddenly, it became a big snake.

Pharaoh's magicians threw their walking sticks down, too. Their walking sticks also became snakes. But Aaron's snake ate all the other snakes.

God had shown Pharaoh a sample of his power. But Pharaoh still would not allow the slaves to be free. Moses warned Pharaoh that God would make terrible things happen if he did not release the slaves. But Pharaoh refused to listen.

Dear God,
Thank you for the place where I worship. I am glad that we are free to worship you wherever we want.
Amen

Food from God

Exodus 16:1

● ●

The Israelites had been slaves in Egypt for many years. God sent Moses to Egypt to set them free. With God's help, Moses led his people out of Egypt. God promised them a new home in the land of Canaan.

But soon after leaving Egypt, the people began complaining to Moses. They were tired and hungry. Some even wanted to return to Egypt where they had

Today's Promise

God cared for the Israelites. He gave them food to eat and water to drink. God promises to supply me with good things to eat, too.

plenty of food to eat.

God heard their complaints. One morning, the Israelites woke up and saw something covering the ground. They did not know what it was. Moses told them that God had sent bread, called *manna*, down from heaven. Each family went out and gathered as much as they needed to eat for the day.

Every morning, manna rained down onto the ground. God continued to send manna to the Israelites until they reached their new home in Canaan.

Dear God,
Thank you for all the good food that I eat every day. Teach me to share with those who do not have enough food.
Amen

God's Ten Rules

Exodus 20:1

• •

Day after day, Moses and the Israelites wandered through the wilderness. They were on their way to their new home in the land of Canaan.

One day, they camped near the bottom of a big mountain. Suddenly, the sky turned dark. Lightning and thunder filled the sky. The mountain was covered with smoke and fire. Everyone was frightened.

Today's Promise

God gave the Israelites special rules to help them. God promises that if I will listen to him, he will teach me right from wrong.

God told Moses to climb to the top of the mountain. Moses told the people not to be afraid. When Moses reached the top, God gave Moses many rules for everyone to obey. These rules would help them live they way they should. God even told Moses how to build a place of worship. It would be a place where people could pray and worship God.

God wrote down ten special rules, or *commandments*, on two stone tablets. He gave them to Moses. Then Moses went down the mountain to give the ten commandments to the people.

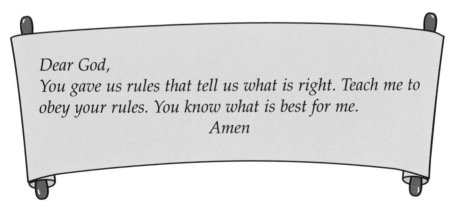

Dear God,
You gave us rules that tell us what is right. Teach me to obey your rules. You know what is best for me.
Amen

Ruth Goes with Naomi

Ruth 1:1

Naomi and her husband lived in Bethlehem. But there was no rain for a long time. So their crops would not grow. They moved to the land of Moab with their two grown sons.

While they lived in Moab, their sons married. One son married a woman named Orpah. The other son married a woman named Ruth.

Today's Promise

Ruth was a loyal friend to Naomi. She stayed with Naomi and helped her. God promises he will always be with me and be my friend.

Later, Naomi's
husband and two
sons died. Naomi,
Ruth, and Orpah
were very sad. Naomi
decided to move back
to Bethlehem to be with
her people. She told
Orpah and Ruth to go back
home to their families.

Orpah and Ruth loved Naomi very much. But Orpah
obeyed Naomi and returned to her family. Ruth refused
to leave Naomi. Ruth knew that it would not be easy
for Naomi to live alone. Ruth said, "Your people shall
be my people, and your God my God."

So Naomi agreed to let Ruth stay with her. They packed up their belongings. They took the long journey back to Bethlehem, where they would begin their new life together.

Ruth worked hard to help Naomi. She went to the fields every day and gathered grain. They used the grain to make flour for bread.

One day, Ruth met the man who owned the field. His name was Boaz. Later, Ruth married Boaz. They cared for Naomi together. Finally, Ruth and Naomi were happy again.

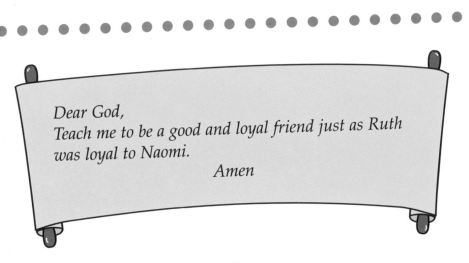

Dear God,
Teach me to be a good and loyal friend just as Ruth
was loyal to Naomi.
Amen

Samuel Hears God

1 Samuel 3:4

Samuel was a young boy who lived at the temple. He helped Eli, who was a priest at the temple. Samuel was also learning about God so that he could be a priest someday.

One night, Samuel was asleep in his bed. He heard a loud voice calling his name. Samuel jumped out of bed and ran to see Eli.

Today's Promise

Samuel listened to God when God spoke to him. God promises to speak to me, too, through the stories in the Bible.

Samuel woke Eli and said, "Here I am."

But Eli did not call Samuel. Eli told him to go back to sleep. So Samuel returned to his bed. The voice spoke to Samuel two more times. And each time, Samuel woke Eli. Finally, Eli told Samuel that God must be calling him.

When Samuel heard the voice again, he said, "Speak, for your servant is listening."

God spoke to Samuel many more times during his life. Samuel grew up to become a prophet. He performed many important jobs for God.

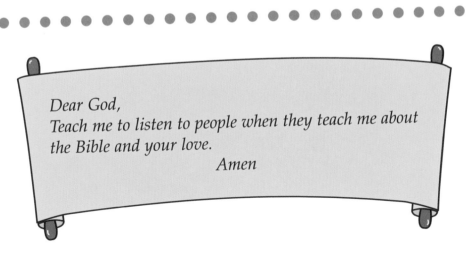

Dear God,
Teach me to listen to people when they teach me about the Bible and your love.
            Amen

Brave Little David

1 Samuel 17:12

• •

David was a shepherd boy. He cared for his family's flock of sheep every day. David's brothers were soldiers in King Saul's army. David wanted to be a soldier, too. But his father told him that he was too young to join the army.

One day, David's father told him to take some food to his brothers. When David found his brothers, he saw

Today's Promise

Little David was brave because he knew God would help him. God promises to help me be brave, too, even when I'm afraid.

an enemy army nearby. Their biggest soldier was a giant named Goliath. Goliath was challenging every soldier in King Saul's army to fight him. But all the king's soldiers were afraid to fight him.

Little David was not afraid. He knew God would protect him from the giant. David went to see the king. David told him that he would fight Goliath. The king gave David his sword and shield and armor to help him. But the king's armor was too big.

David knew what to do. He found some stones in a stream. He gathered five small stones and placed them in his pouch. Then he faced the giant with his stones and his sling. Goliath laughed when he saw David.

The giant became angry and walked toward him. David placed one of the small stones in his sling and swung it over his head. The stone flew through the air and hit the giant on his forehead. The giant fell to the ground. With God's help, little David defeated Goliath. And he saved King Saul's army.

Dear God,
Sometimes, I am afraid when I meet kids I don't know.
Teach me to be brave so I can make new friends.
Amen

David's Best Friend

1 Samuel 18:1

Affter David defeated the giant, Goliath, King Saul invited David to live at his palace. David was very happy there for a while. He met Saul's son Jonathan, and they became good friends.

David became a leader in Saul's army and won many battles. After a while, Saul became so jealous of David that Saul tried to kill him. So David ran away.

Today's Promise

Jonathan was David's good friend even when Saul became jealous of David. God promises that he will always be my friend, too, and he will never leave me.

David hid inside a cave. Jonathan found him and came to see him. Jonathan promised David that he would talk to his father. He would ask King Saul if David could return to the palace.

Jonathan kept his promise. He asked his father to allow David to come back. But King Saul was still jealous of David.

Sadly, Jonathan warned David that King Saul would not let him return. David and Jonathan said good-bye to each other. Then David went far away so that Saul could not find him.

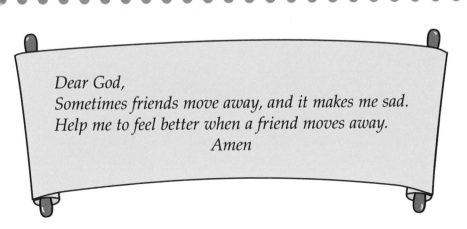

Dear God,
Sometimes friends move away, and it makes me sad.
Help me to feel better when a friend moves away.
Amen

David Becomes King

2 Samuel 2:4

When David was a boy, the prophet Samuel anointed him and told him that God had chosen him to be the king of Israel someday. After that, David went to live at the palace with King Saul. At first, David and Saul were good friends. Then Saul became angry at David and chased him from the palace. David wandered from place to place for a long time.

Today's Promise

David waited a long time to become king of Israel. God promises that if I have patience, he will answer my prayers, too.

One day, King Saul was killed in a battle with an enemy army. Saul's enemies captured many parts of Israel. David would have to defeat them before he could be the king of Israel.

So David led his own soldiers to fight the enemy armies. With God's help, David's army defeated them and saved the people of Israel.

David called for a great celebration to praise God. The people sang and danced and played music. After waiting a long time, David had finally become the king of Israel.

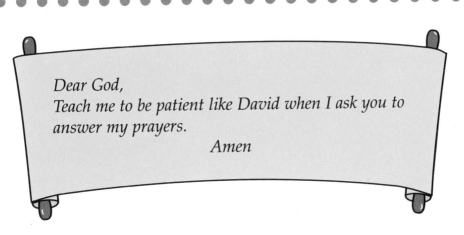

Dear God,
Teach me to be patient like David when I ask you to answer my prayers.
Amen

Elisha's New Friends

2 Kings 4:8

Elisha was a prophet. He traveled to many places and talked to people about God. One day, a rich woman invited Elisha to her house for dinner.

The woman and her husband became Elisha's good friends. Each time Elisha came to town, they would invite him to their home for a meal.

The woman and her husband even built a small

Today's Promise

Elisha's friends were kind to him. And Elisha gave them a special gift. God is kind and promises to do special things for me, too.

room on top of their house where Elisha could stay.

One day, Elisha went up to his room to rest. He thought about the kind man and woman. He wanted to do something special for them.

Elisha asked his helper what he should do. His helper told him that the couple did not have any children. So Elisha told the woman that God was going to bless them with a son.

The woman was shocked. She could hardly believe what she was hearing. But, several months later, the woman gave birth to a baby boy.

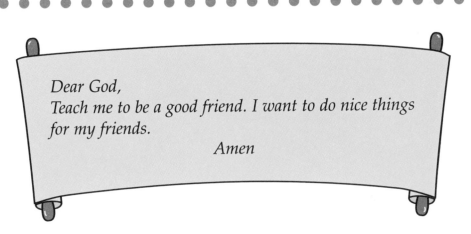

Dear God,
Teach me to be a good friend. I want to do nice things for my friends.
Amen

Brave Esther

Esther 2:17

●●●●●●●●●●●●●●●●●●●●●●●●

The king of Persia was looking for someone to become his queen. He ordered his best helpers to search the kingdom for any woman who might be his bride. The king's helpers brought many women to the palace to meet the king.

The king met some of the most beautiful women in the kingdom. But he was not pleased with any of them.

Today's Promise

Esther was brave to face the king. God promises to give me courage to always do the right thing.

Then a young
Jewish woman
named Esther came
to the palace to meet
the king. She was the
most beautiful
woman he had ever
seen. And Esther was
very wise. The king married
Esther and made her the queen
over his kingdom.

One day, Haman, the king's best helper, ordered all
Jewish people to bow to him. But Esther's cousin,
Mordecai, refused to bow down to Haman. This made
Haman very angry. So Haman paid the king a lot of

money to pass a new law. This law would allow Haman
to get rid of all the Jewish people in the kingdom.

When Esther heard about the new law, she went to
see the king. Esther was very brave. She told him that
she was Jewish. And she begged him not to harm her
people. The king was very angry that Haman had
tricked him.

The king changed the law. Brave
Queen Esther saved her people.
Then the king had Haman arrested
for tricking him. And Mordecai
became the king's new helper.

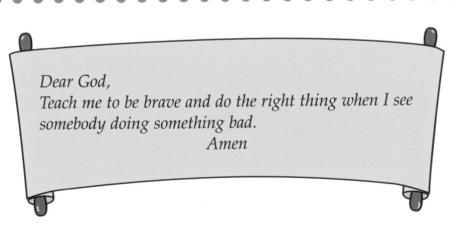

Dear God,
Teach me to be brave and do the right thing when I see
somebody doing something bad.
                    Amen

Nehemiah Rebuilds

Nehemiah 2:17

• •

The Israelites had been driven from Jerusalem by an enemy army. Every building in the city had been damaged. Even the walls around the city had been knocked down. So, many Israelites moved to Persia. They lived there for many years.

Nehemiah was an Israelite who worked for the king of Persia. He learned that some Israelites were moving

Today's Promise

Nehemiah worked hard to rebuild the walls around Jerusalem. God promises to help me do my best, too.

back to Jerusalem. They were cleaning up the city and repairing their homes. But nobody had rebuilt the walls around the city.

Nehemiah wanted the walls to be rebuilt. He prayed to God and asked him for help. The king saw that Nehemiah was very sad. So the king allowed him to return to Jerusalem.

Nehemiah went there right away. He gathered a group of people to help him. He told them what needed to be done. They all worked very hard and quickly rebuilt the walls.

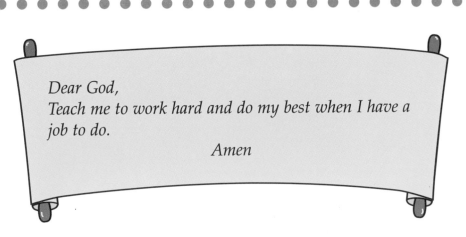

Dear God,
Teach me to work hard and do my best when I have a job to do.

Amen

Three Men in a Fire

Daniel 3:12

The king of Babylon did not worship God. He had a golden statue built for people to worship. Anyone in his kingdom who did not bow down to the statue would be punished.

Shadrach, Meshach, and Abednego worked for the king. They worshiped God. They would not bow down to the golden statue. This made the king very angry. He

Today's Promise

Shadrach, Meshach, and Abednego worshiped God even when others did not. God protected them in the fire. God promises to protect me, too.

had them brought to the palace to see him.

The king told the three men that they must bow down to the golden statue or they would be punished. The three men refused to obey the king. So the king had them thrown into a very hot furnace.

Then something wonderful happened! Suddenly there were four men in the furnace instead of three. The hot fire was not harming them at all. God had sent an angel to protect the three men. So the king removed them from the furnace. He announced that their God was the only true God.

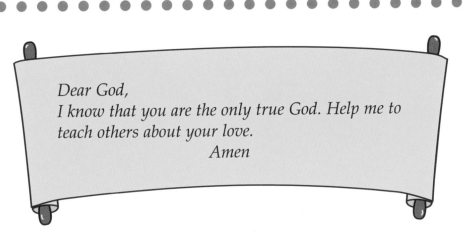

Dear God,
I know that you are the only true God. Help me to teach others about your love.
Amen

Daniel and the Lions

Daniel 6:3

King Darius ruled over a large kingdom. He chose Daniel to be his best helper. The king's other helpers were jealous of Daniel. So they tried to get rid of him.

They spied on Daniel and saw him praying to God every day. They came up with a plan. The helpers tricked the king into signing a new law. This law said

Today's Promise

Daniel prayed to God every day, even when it was not easy for him. God heard his prayers and helped him. God promises to hear my prayers, too.

that all people must pray to the king. They were not allowed to pray to God.

But Daniel prayed to God anyway. The king liked Daniel, but he had to obey the law. So the king had Daniel thrown into the lions' den.

The next morning, the king went to see if Daniel was all right. God had sent an angel to protect him. The king was very happy. Daniel was freed from the lions' den. The king realized that God had saved Daniel. The king changed the law and told everyone to worship God.

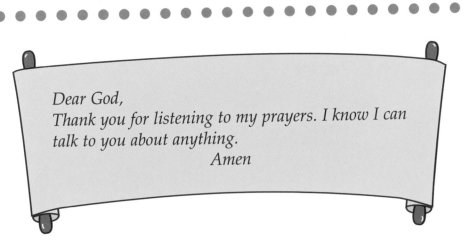

Dear God,
Thank you for listening to my prayers. I know I can talk to you about anything.
Amen

Jonah and the Big Fish

Jonah 1:1-2

● ●

One day, God told Jonah to go to Nineveh. Jonah could teach the people about God. But Jonah did not like the people of Nineveh.

So Jonah tried to run away from God. Jonah hid on a ship that was sailing out to sea. But God found Jonah and sent a big storm. The sailors on the ship were frightened. Jonah knew that God had sent the storm. So

Today's Promise

After the fish spit him out, Jonah told the people of Nineveh about God. God promises to help me tell others about how much he loves all of us.

Jonah told the sailors to throw him into the sea.

The sailors threw Jonah off the ship. Then the storm stopped. God sent a big fish to swallow Jonah. Jonah stayed inside the fish for three days. He told God that he was sorry for running away. God forgave Jonah.

The fish spit out Jonah onto the shore. Jonah went right away to the city of Nineveh. He told the people to love God and worship him. The king and all the people of Nineveh were happy that Jonah came to see them.

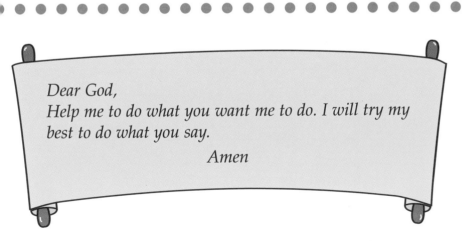

Dear God,
Help me to do what you want me to do. I will try my
best to do what you say.

Amen

Mary Is Chosen

Luke 1:26-27

Mary was a young woman living in the tiny town of Nazareth. Mary loved God very much. One day, the angel Gabriel came to visit Mary. She was frightened by the strange visitor.

The angel told Mary not to be afraid. God had sent him to give her a special message. God had chosen her from all other women to give birth to his only son.

Today's Promise

God chose Mary to have his son. Mary was special to God. God promises to love me always. He says that I am special, too.

Gabriel told Mary that the baby's name would be Jesus.

At first, Mary did not understand Gabriel's message. She was not even married. She was engaged to marry a young carpenter named Joseph. Mary did not know how she could be the mother of God's son.

But the angel told her that God could do anything. Gabriel said, "He will be great, and will be called the Son of the Most High." Mary told the angel she was happy that God had chosen her to have his son. Then the angel left Mary.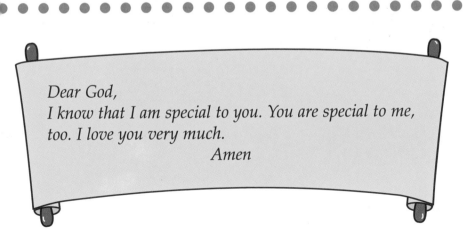

Dear God,
I know that I am special to you. You are special to me, too. I love you very much.
Amen

John Talks about Jesus

Matthew 3:1-2

An angel had told Mary that she was going to have God's son. The same angel had told Elizabeth that she was going to have a son, too. His name would be John.

When John grew up, he lived in the wilderness. He loved God very much. And he knew that Jesus was God's son. God gave John a very important job. John

Today's Promise

John was happy to tell people about Jesus. God promises that Jesus will always love me and live in my heart.

talked to people about Jesus. He told them that Jesus was God's son. Jesus would teach people about God and forgive their sins.

Many people believed John's message. They told God that they were sorry for doing bad things. They also accepted Jesus as God's son.

Then John baptized them. He led them down to the river. He dipped them under the water and lifted them up again. The people were ready to live the way God wanted them to live. And they could tell others about Jesus, too.

Dear God,
Help me learn more about Jesus. I love Jesus because he is your son and because he loves me, too.
                    Amen

Jesus Passes a Test

Matthew 4:1

● ●

Jesus had spent his childhood with his parents, Mary and Joseph. Now he was a man. It was time for him to tell people that he was God's son. He was also going to teach people about God. And he would use his power to heal people who were sick.

But first, Jesus went to the desert to be alone and to pray to God. He stayed there for forty days without

Today's Promise

Sometimes friends tempt me to do things I know I shouldn't do. God promises to give me the strength to do what's right when I'm tempted.

any food or water. Satan found Jesus alone in the desert and decided to trick him into doing something bad.

Satan saw that Jesus was hungry and thirsty. So Satan told Jesus to use his powers to turn stones into bread. Jesus said he did not need to eat. God was taking care of him.

Then Satan offered Jesus the world if Jesus would worship him. But Jesus knew that the world belongs to God. Jesus told Satan that he should worship God. Satan stopped testing Jesus and left him alone.

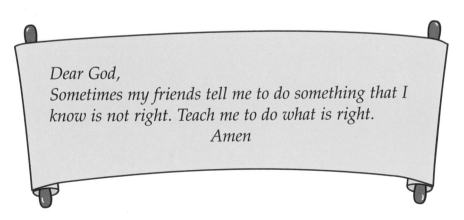

Dear God,
Sometimes my friends tell me to do something that I know is not right. Teach me to do what is right.
Amen

Jesus Chooses Disciples

Matthew 4:18

Jesus was ready to teach people about God. But he knew he could not do it alone. He needed help to reach lots of people. He began to look for people who would follow him. They would travel with him to many places. And they would be his friends.

Jesus walked to a lake. He saw two fishermen. Peter and his brother, Andrew, were trying to catch fish with

Today's Promise

Jesus' disciples followed him to many places. He taught them about God. God promises to help me follow Jesus, too.

nets. Jesus told them to put down their nets and follow him. They were going to help him teach people about God. The two men quickly obeyed Jesus.

Later, Jesus met two more fishermen. James and his brother, John, were repairing a net. They left their nets behind and followed Jesus, too.

Jesus selected twelve men to be his helpers. They were called his disciples. Jesus taught them many things about God's love. They followed him and learned to serve God.

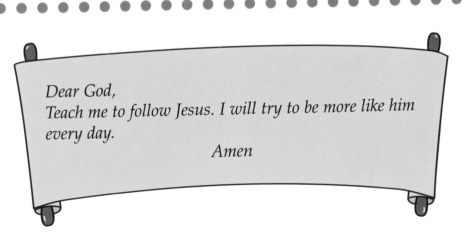

Dear God,
Teach me to follow Jesus. I will try to be more like him every day.

Amen

Helping a
Sick Friend

Mark 2:1-2

Jesus had only been preaching for a short time. But many people already believed that he was God's son. He taught people about God's love. And he healed people who were very sick just by touching them or speaking to them.

Soon, big crowds followed Jesus wherever he went. Once, Jesus was preaching to a group of people inside a

Today's Promise

The four men were good friends to the sick man. God promises to help me be a good friend, too.

house. The house quickly filled up. More people came and stood outside.

Four men had a friend who could not walk. They brought him to Jesus to be healed. But the crowd would not let them near Jesus. So the men lifted their sick friend to the roof of the house on a mat. They removed part of the roof and gently lowered their friend to Jesus. Jesus told the sick man that his sins were forgiven. Then Jesus told him to stand up, pick up his mat, and go home. The man was healed! Everyone was amazed at Jesus' healing power.

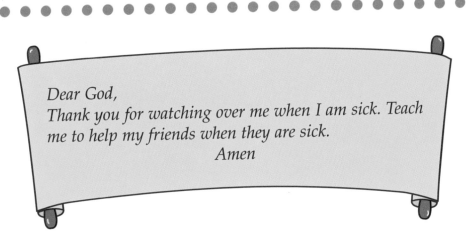

Dear God,
Thank you for watching over me when I am sick. Teach me to help my friends when they are sick.
Amen

Jesus Calms a Storm

Matthew 8:23

Jesus had chosen twelve men to be his disciples. They helped him teach people about God. They also helped him heal sick people. Large crowds often came to meet Jesus and hear his words.

Jesus had already taught the disciples many things. But they still did not understand that Jesus had the power of God to do many great things.

Today's Promise

Jesus cared for the disciples and kept them safe from harm. God promises to take care of me, too.

One day, Jesus had been teaching a large group of people. Jesus and the disciples left to find a quiet place to rest. They climbed into a boat and went out on a lake. Then Jesus fell asleep.

Suddenly, a terrible storm came. It shook the boat. The disciples were afraid. They woke Jesus because they thought the boat was going to sink.

Jesus said, "Peace! Be still!"

The storm stopped. The disciples were amazed at what they saw.

Jesus told them that they should always trust him.

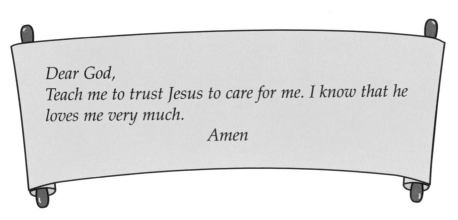

Dear God,
Teach me to trust Jesus to care for me. I know that he
loves me very much.
                    Amen

The Poor Woman's Gift

Mark 12:41-42

Jesus often went to the temple to pray to God. One day, the temple was crowded with people who came to worship God. Jesus sat down and watched people as they brought gifts of money to the temple.

Priests at the temple used the money to care for the temple building. They also used the money to help other people.

Today's Promise

The poor woman gave everything she had to God. God promises to bless me when I give my time or money to him.

Jesus watched as rich people offered bags of gold and silver coins at the temple. They had lots of money and were dressed in fine clothes.

Then Jesus saw a poor woman arrive at the temple. Her husband had died, and she lived alone. She offered two coins at the temple. Jesus knew this was all the money that the woman had for food.

Jesus told his disciples that the poor woman's gift was more special than the money given by the rich people. She had given all the money she had to God.

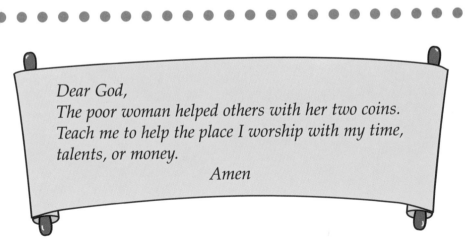

Dear God,
The poor woman helped others with her two coins.
Teach me to help the place I worship with my time,
talents, or money.

Amen

One Lost Sheep

Luke 15:4

Jesus traveled to many places to teach people about God. Jesus loved everyone, and he taught anyone who wanted to hear his words.

This made some men very angry. They saw Jesus teaching people who had never worshiped God. They saw Jesus teaching people who had done many bad things.

Today's Promise

Jesus loved all people. He taught about God to anyone who wanted to listen. God promises to teach me when I listen.

So Jesus told these men a story. A shepherd had one hundred sheep. He cared for all his sheep. But one sheep became lost. The shepherd searched and searched until he found the lost sheep.

Jesus explained that the one sheep that was lost was like one person who did not believe in God. Or it might be a person who had done many bad things. The rest of the sheep were like people who already loved God. The people who were like the lost sheep needed to hear about God's love more than people who already worshiped God.

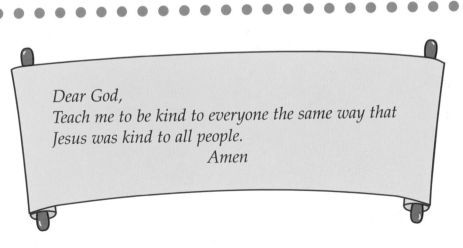

Dear God,
Teach me to be kind to everyone the same way that Jesus was kind to all people.
Amen

A Boy Shares His Lunch

John 6:11

• •

One day, a huge crowd came to see Jesus. He preached to them, and he healed the people who were sick. Jesus stayed with them all day.

In the evening, the people were getting hungry. And the disciples had no food to share with them. So the disciples told Jesus that he should send the people home. But Jesus told the disciples to feed the people.

Today's Promise

One boy helped many people by sharing his food with Jesus. God promises to help me to share what I have with my friends and family.

One boy had five loaves of bread and two fish. He shared his food with Jesus. The disciples told Jesus that this was not enough to feed the crowd. But Jesus knew what to do.

First Jesus told everyone to sit down. Then he prayed over the food and broke it into pieces. The disciples gave the food to the crowd. There was plenty of food for everyone. Jesus had performed a miracle! After the people had finished eating, the disciples gathered the food that was left. There were twelve baskets of fish and bread!

Dear God,
One boy helped many people because he shared his food.
Teach me to share what I have with others.
                    Amen

Jesus Walks on Water

Matthew 14:22

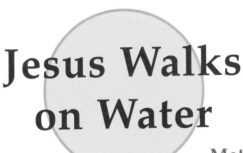

After Jesus finished preaching to a group of people, he led his disciples to a lake. The disciples climbed into a boat. They waited for Jesus while he went up to a mountain to pray. Then a storm came. It pushed the boat far away from shore.

Later, Jesus returned to the lake. He walked on the water to reach the boat! The disciples saw someone

Today's Promise

Jesus taught the disciples to have faith in him because he could do anything. God promises that when I have faith in him, he will help me to do all kinds of things.

walking toward them. They thought it was a ghost.
They were afraid. When Jesus came closer to the boat,
the disciples were amazed to see him on the water.

Peter trusted Jesus so much that he hopped out of
the boat. He walked toward Jesus on the water. But
Peter looked away from Jesus and saw the dark clouds
and the big waves. He became frightened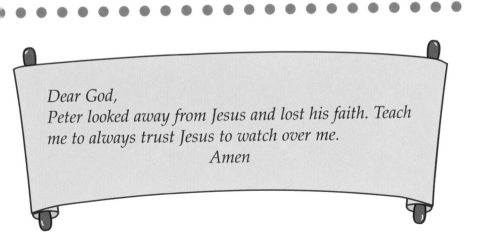
and began to sink. Jesus reached down
and helped him back into the boat.

Jesus told Peter to always have faith
in him. Jesus would care for him and
the other disciples.

Dear God,
Peter looked away from Jesus and lost his faith. Teach
me to always trust Jesus to watch over me.
Amen

Story of the Hurt Man

Luke 10:27

Jesus taught people to love God and worship him. He also taught people to love their neighbors. To help people understand this, he told a story.

One day, a man was walking along the road. Suddenly, a group of thieves attacked him. They hurt him and took his money. Then they ran away and left him on the road.

Today's Promise

The good Samaritan was kind to his neighbor. God promises to help me be nice to my neighbors, too.

Another man walked along the same road. He saw the hurt man. But he did not help the hurt stranger. Instead, he crossed to the other side of the road. And he left the hurt man alone. Then another man walked by. He would not stop to help either.

Finally, a man from Samaria was walking along the road and saw the hurt stranger. The Samaritan helped him. The kind Samaritan bandaged the stranger's wounds and took him to a nice place to stay.

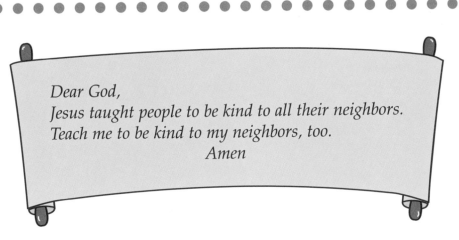

Dear God,
Jesus taught people to be kind to all their neighbors.
Teach me to be kind to my neighbors, too.
Amen

Listening to Jesus

Luke 10:38

• •

Jesus had many good friends and followers. Some of them traveled with him. They watched him teach other people about God. They also helped Jesus in many ways.

Mary, Martha, and their brother Lazarus were some of Jesus' best friends. Whenever Jesus traveled through their village, they welcomed him into their home.

Today's Promise

Mary knew that it was important to listen to Jesus. God promises to teach me to listen not only with my head but with my heart, too.

One day, Jesus was visiting Mary and Martha at their house. Jesus sat with Mary and talked to her about God's love. Mary listened quietly to Jesus' words of wisdom.

Martha was too busy to listen to Jesus. She had lots of housework to finish. She was probably cleaning the house or cooking a special meal for their guest.

Martha complained to Jesus that Mary should be helping her with the chores. Jesus told her that she should be listening to his lessons instead of worrying about other things.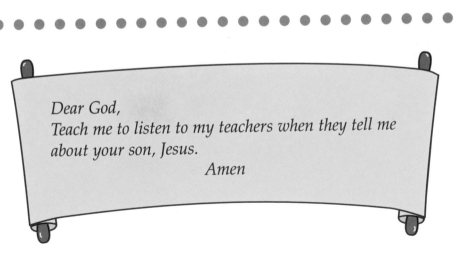

Dear God,
Teach me to listen to my teachers when they tell me about your son, Jesus.
                    Amen

Story of the Prodigal Son

Luke 15:11-12

● ●

Jesus often told stories called *parables* to help people understand God's love. Jesus told one story about a young man who lived with his father and his brother.

One day, the young man asked his father for some money. He wanted to travel and see the world. The young man's father gave him the money for his trip.

Today's Promise

The young man's father forgave his son for wasting all his money. I promise to ask God to forgive me when I do something bad.

The young man spent lots of money on fancy clothes and fine food. Soon all the money was gone. The young man had to get a job feeding pigs. He was very sad.

The young man missed his family. He returned home. He told his father he was sorry for wasting all his money. His father was very happy that he had returned home safely. His father forgave him for spending all his money. He even gave his son a party to welcome him home.

Jesus was saying that God is like a loving father. When we are sorry for doing bad things, he always forgives us.

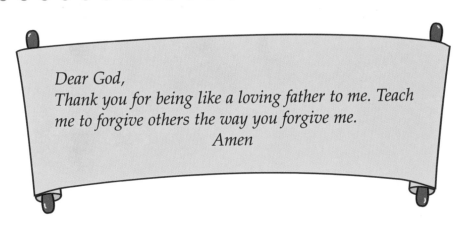

Dear God,
Thank you for being like a loving father to me. Teach me to forgive others the way you forgive me.
Amen

Jesus and the Children

Matthew 19:13

● ●

Jesus traveled to many places. He met lots of people. He talked to all kinds of people. Some people were rich. Some people were very poor.

Jesus also met many people who were sick. He could heal them by just talking to them or touching them. He healed people who could not see. He healed people who had never been able to walk before.

Today's Promise

Jesus loves children all over the world. God promises that Jesus loves me, too. No matter where I go, Jesus will always go with me.

161

Sometimes Jesus taught people and healed sick people all day. One day, some families brought their children to meet Jesus. The disciples told them to go away. Jesus was too tired to visit with the children, they said.

Jesus saw what the disciples were doing. He told them to let the children come to him. The children were very happy to see Jesus. He was happy to see them, too. Jesus hugged each child. He told them that he loved them all very much. Then Jesus said that everyone should trust God the way children trust him.

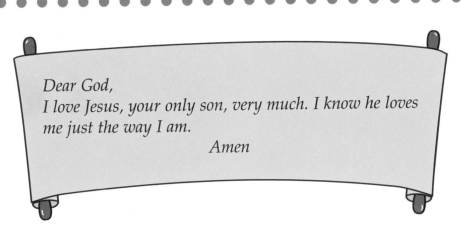

Dear God,
I love Jesus, your only son, very much. I know he loves me just the way I am.
Amen

Trouble in the Temple

John 2:13-14

• •

Jesus arrived in Jerusalem just before Passover. Many people were coming to the city for the holy festival. During the festival, they would visit the temple to worship God and pray.

Jesus went to the temple to pray. But when he arrived at the temple, he did not see people worshiping God. The temple was filled with merchants. They were

Today's Promise

Jesus told the merchants that they should respect the place where they worship God. God promises to be close to me when I worship.

using the temple as a place to sell their goods. They were selling things like cows and sheep and birds.

This made Jesus very angry. First he chased the animals out of the temple. Then he knocked over the merchants' tables. Finally, he poured their money onto the floor.

Jesus told the merchants that the temple was a holy place. It was not a place to sell their goods. He said they had turned it into "a den of robbers." Then Jesus left Jerusalem with his disciples.

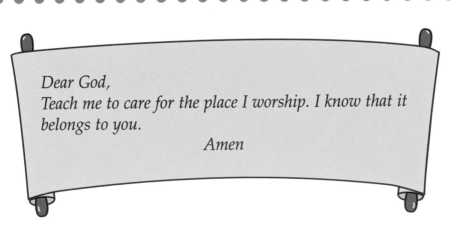

Dear God,
Teach me to care for the place I worship. I know that it belongs to you.

Amen

Jesus Returns

● ●

Many people loved Jesus. They knew that he was God's son. But some people did not follow Jesus. They wanted to get rid of him.

Jesus' enemies had him arrested and killed. His friends buried him in a tomb and covered it with a stone. Then his enemies placed guards in front of the tomb to keep people away.

Today's Promise

I know that Jesus died and came back to life again. God promises that Jesus is alive in heaven.

One day, some of Jesus' friends went to see his tomb. Suddenly, the earth shook. An angel appeared and rolled the stone away. The guards saw the angel and fell to the ground. The angel told Jesus' friends not to be afraid. They looked inside the tomb. Jesus was gone!

His friends left to tell the disciples what had happened. But on the way, they met Jesus. He was alive again! Jesus' friends were very happy to see him. They bowed down and worshiped him. Then Jesus told them to find his disciples and tell them the good news.

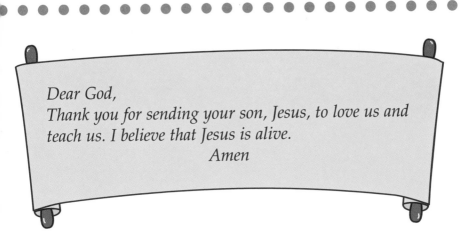

Dear God,
Thank you for sending your son, Jesus, to love us and teach us. I believe that Jesus is alive.
Amen

Paul Takes a Trip

Acts 13:1-2

● ●

Before he believed in Jesus' teachings, Paul hated Jesus' followers. But now he loved Jesus, too. Paul taught other people about God's son. He helped start a church so people could worship together.

While Paul and others were worshiping at their church, God spoke to them. God told them to send Paul and his friend Barnabas on a long journey.

Today's Promise

Paul and his friend taught many people about Jesus. God promises to help me read my Bible stories and learn more about Jesus, too.

Paul and Barnabas traveled to many cities. They taught many people about Jesus. God even gave Paul the power to heal people. In one city, Paul met a man who had never been able to walk. Paul told him to stand up. The man instantly stood up and walked!

Some people did not believe what the two men told them. They tried to kill Paul and Barnabas. But God watched over them. Paul and Barnabas did not give up. Many people listened to them. With God's help, the two men started new churches where people learned about Jesus.

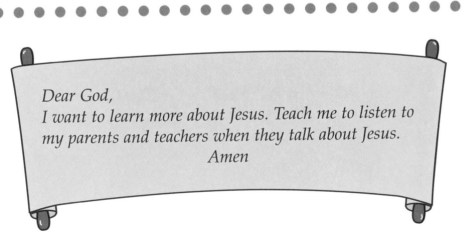

Dear God,
I want to learn more about Jesus. Teach me to listen to
my parents and teachers when they talk about Jesus.
Amen

If you have enjoyed this book or if it has impacted your life, we would like to hear from you. Please contact us at:

Honor Books
Department E
P.O. Box 55388
Tulsa, Oklahoma 74155

Or by e-mail at info@honorbooks.com

Additional copies of this book and other Honor Books titles are available from your local bookstore.